W9-BAJ-205

I am an ARO PUBLISHING
TEN WORD BOOK

My ten words are:

I	mushroom
wonder	web
what	leaf
this	fish
is	wonderworm

Wonder Worm

10 WORDS

Story by Bob and Brittany Reese

Pictures by Bob Reese

ISBN 0-89868-249-5--Library Bound
ISBN 0-89868-250-9--Soft Bound
Spanish ISBN 0-89868-257-6--Library Bound
Spanish ISBN 0-89868-258-4--Soft Bound

I
wonder
what
this
is?

Mushroom!

I
wonder
what
this
is?

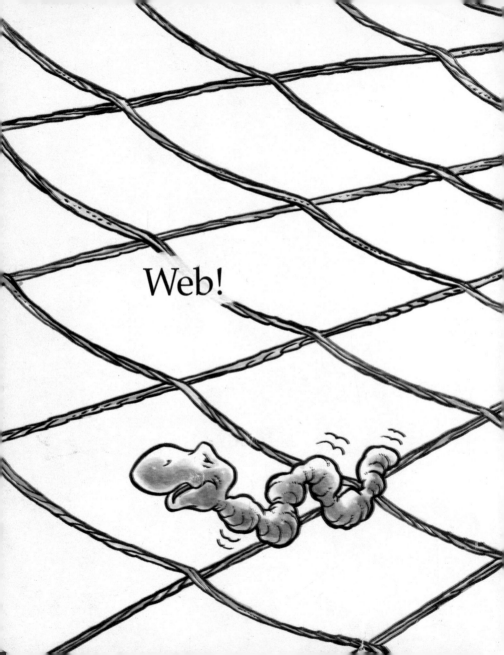

I
wonder
what
this
is?

Leaf!

I
wonder
what
this
is?

Fish!

I
wonder
what
this
is?

Wonderworm!

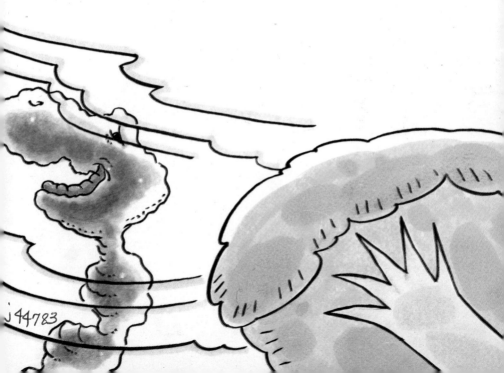

j 44783

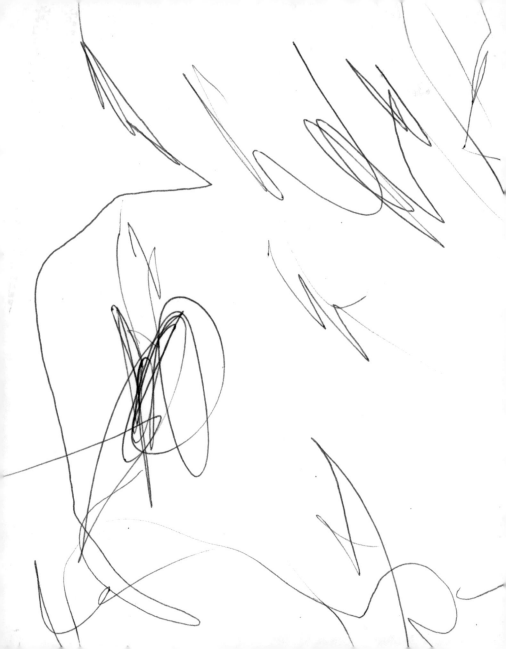